Collins
MUSIC

UKULELE
MAGIC

SONGBOOK

IAN LAWRENCE

First published 2018
Published by Collins, an imprint of HarperCollins*Publishers* Ltd
The News Building
1 London Bridge Street
London Bridge
SE1 9GF

www.collins.co.uk

© 2018 HarperCollins*Publishers* Ltd

ISBN: 978-1-4729-2919-8

Text and music © 2018 Ian Lawrence
Printed by Caligraving Ltd, Thetford, Norfolk
Designed by Ken Vail Graphic Design Ltd
Vocals performed by Daisy Moon, Frances Lea and Ian Lawrence
Sound engineering by Stephen Chadwick

MIX
Paper from
responsible sources
FSC™ C007454

This book is produced from independently certified FSC paper
to ensure responsible forest management.

For more information visit: **www.harpercollins.co.uk/green**

Contents

Welcome to
Ukulele Magic Songbook

Diagrams show what strings to play and where to put your fingers.

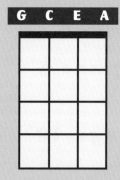

Use the tuning track to tune your ukulele strings.

fingertips

The fingertips text tells you how to play and what you need to know to play well.

Ukulele Magic Songbook offers an array of fun and varied tunes that will help you and your pupils consolidate basic chords and techniques, including all those introduced in *Ukulele Magic Tutor Book*. As well as strumming chords, there are tips for singing the songs, playing the melody lines using the leadsheets and TAB scores provided, creating new words and tunes, and performing songs as rounds – ideal for developing every aspect of musicianship.

Audio support

The CD provides a demo and backing track for every song in *Ukulele Magic Songbook*, along with a tuning track. Choose to sing or play along with the demo for support, or go solo using the backing track. Where needed, backing tracks start with percussion 'count-in' beats so that you know when to start playing.

 Tuning track

Leadsheets

Leadsheets of every song are provided as printable PDFs on the CD. These scores include the melody line, chord names, the main song lyrics, and instructions for performing (e.g. as a round).

TAB sheets

The CD also contains TAB sheets for selected songs, as indicated in the book. This gives players the opportunity to play simple melodies on the ukulele while developing their TAB reading.

On Track xx/xx
An explanation of the song structure and any important features of the CD tracks.

Challenge
Further ideas to develop the song and learn new skills.

Songfacts
Background information to help you put the song in context.

UNIT 1
OPEN STRINGS

FOUR SONGS TO SING AND PLAY

Church bells

Friendships

I'm going home

Cowboy song

In this section you will:

- Play four songs that only use the open strings (G, C, E, A)
- Practise the thumb rest stroke and the thumb brush strum
- Play the open strings in different orders

Things to remember:

When playing the open strings, it is important that they 'ring' clearly, so try not to touch the string accidentally after you have played it.

- Be careful to support the neck of the ukulele without touching any of the strings with your left hand.
- Make sure that only the thumb of your right hand has contact with the strings, not any other fingers or the palm of your hand.
- Roll up your sleeves to avoid them accidentally touching the strings as you play.

This section supports Unit 1 (Meet my ukulele) in the *Ukulele Magic Tutor Book.*

Church bells

Open strings

G C E A

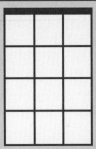

fingertips

● For each verse, play the open strings in the same order: G C E A.

● Use the thumb 'rest stroke' (▼) : your thumb should come to rest on the next string (see *Ukulele Magic Tutor Book*, page 4).

● At the end the clock strikes seven. Play seven strums on the open string.

VERSE

1. Hear those church bells sing their song.

   ▼   ▼   ▼   ▼   ▼   ▼   ▼

   G   C   E   A   G   C   E

CHORUS

Ding, dong, ding, dong

▼   ▼   ▼   ▼

A   G   C   E

Ding, dang, dong!

▼   ▼   ▼

A   G   C

2. Sun-day morn-ing comes a-long. (to CHORUS)

   ▼   ▼   ▼   ▼   ▼   ▼   ▼

   G   C   E   A   G   C   E

ENDING

▼ ▼ ▼ ▼ ▼ ▼ ▼

1 2 3 4 5 6 7

On track

After a 4-bar introduction, the verses and chorus are played three times:

● First time: sing
● Second time: play
● Third time: sing and play (with the ending)

Challenge

● Make up your own open-string tune to play to these words. Try playing the strings in a few different orders and hear what sounds good.

Songfacts

This song was specially written to help you to remember the letter names of the open strings.

Open strings

G C E A

Of tall ships and small ships and all ships at sea,
▼ ▼ ▼ ▼ ▼ ▼ ▼ ▼▼ ▼ ▼
G G G G C C C E E A G

All ships at sea, all ships at sea,
▼ ▼ ▼ ▼ ▼ ▼ ▼ ▼
C E A G C E A G

The best ships are friendships and long may they be,
▼ ▼ ▼ ▼ ▼ ▼ ▼ ▼ ▼ ▼ ▼
G G G G C C C E E A G

Long may they be, yes long may they be!
▼ ▼ ▼ ▼ ▼ ▼ ▼ ▼ ▼
C E A G C E A G C

fingertips

● Remember to use the thumb rest stroke and avoid touching the strings while they are ringing.

● Be especially careful with repeated notes.

On track

3/4

The version on the CD is in the style of an Irish folk band. After a 4-bar introduction the song is heard three times. The second verse is instrumental.

Challenge

● Compose (make up) your own melody for the song, keeping to the same order of open strings. Your new tune may not fit with the backing track but you could play it as an unaccompanied solo.

Songfacts

Like *Church bells*, the strings are played in the same order throughout, G C E A, but some notes are repeated. The words are from an Irish 'toast' to friendship.

I'm going home

Open strings

G	C	E	A

I've travelled far; a wand'ring soul.

▼ ▼ ▼ ▼ ▼ ▼ ▼ ▼

C C A G C C A G

I've seen the world from West to East, and Pole to Pole.

▼ ▼ ▼ ▼ ▼ ▼ ▼ ▼ ▼ ▼ ▼ ▼

C C A G A G E G A G E G

All roads, they say, will lead to Rome

▼ ▼ ▼ ▼ ▼ ▼ ▼ ▼

C C A G C C A G

But not the road I'm on today; I'm going home.

▼ ▼ ▼ ▼ ▼ ▼ ▼ ▼ ▼ ▼ ▼ ▼

C C A G A G E G E G E C

fingertips

● Play this song using the thumb rest stroke.

● There is a longer note at the end of each musical phrase. Let the strings ring on these longer notes by not touching (or 'damping') them accidentally with your hands or shirt sleeves.

On track

5/6

There is a 3-bar introduction on the backing track and then the song is played three times:

● First time: sing
● Second time: play
● Third time: sing and play

Challenge

● Try composing your own song. Take the words and the rhythm from this song, but change the order of the open strings to create a new tune.

● Your tune may not fit with the backing track, but you can play it as a solo piece.

Songfacts

Many thoughtful songs have been written about travelling and returning home.

Listen to *Homeward bound* by Paul Simon, *Country roads* by John Denver or the Beatles' song *The long and winding road*.

Cowboy song

Open strings

G	C	E	A

VERSE

On the Chis - holm Trail, Drov - ers rode a - long
▼   ▼   ▼   ▼   ▼   ▼   ▼   ▼   ▼
C   E   C   E   C   C   E   C   E   C

Herd - ing cat - tle as they sang a cow-boy song. **(last time to ENDING)**
C   E   C   E   C   E   C   E   G   E   C

Though the work was hard, and the days were long,
C   E   C   E   C   C   E   C   E   C

Round the fire at night they sang a cow-boy song.
C   E   C   E   C   E   C   E   G   E   C

BRIDGE

Six-ty days to Kan-sas, where the grass is green.
A   A   A   A   A   A   A   A   G   E   G

Tex-as, Ok-la-ho-ma, on to A-be-line. **(to VERSE)**
A   A   A   A   A   A   A   A   G   E   G

ENDING

Herd - ing cat - tle as they sang a cow-boy song.
C   E   C   E   C   E   C   E   G   E   C

fingertips

● The melody of this song should be 'thumb picked' using the thumb rest stroke to produce a rich, full tone.

7/8 On track

● On the track there is a 4-bar introduction before the song is sung all the way through.

● Use the backing track to accompany the song as a ukulele solo.

Challenge

● Check out some famous old American cowboy songs like *The streets of Laredo*, *Home on the range*, *Red river valley* and *Get along, little dogies*.

Songfacts

In the USA, between 1866 and 1886, 20 million cattle were herded from Texas to Kansas where they would be loaded on to trains to stockyards in Chicago.

On these cattle trails, the cowboys discovered that singing or whistling songs as they rode along would keep the cattle calm. Many of these songs were composed by the cowboys themselves. They would also be sung in the evening, round the campfires.

UNIT 2
ONE-CHORD SONGS

FIVE SONGS TO SING AND PLAY

Vamos a remar (Row, row, row your boat)

Tongo

Ah, poor bird

Fly away

Engine number nine

In this section you will:

- Play five songs using only one chord for each song

- Practise different strumming patterns using your thumb and first finger

- Practise songs that can be sung in two parts: an 'echo song' and a 'round'

- Have the opportunity to play the tune of a song using TAB notation

Things to remember:

- Strum each chord before you begin the song.

- Make sure you are using the correct fingers and pressing your fingertips down firmly onto the strings.

- Check that all four strings are ringing clearly. If a string sounds dull it may be because you are accidentally touching it and 'damping' the sound.

- Remember to roll up those sleeves.

This section supports these Units of the *Ukulele Magic Tutor Book*:

- *Vamos a remar* and *Tongo* – Unit 3 (Our first chord)

- *Ah Poor Bird'* – Unit 4 (A minor miracle)

- *Fly away* – Unit 5 (All change)

- *Engine number nine* – Unit 6 (Three chord tricks)

Check it out!

Here are some one-chord songs you could try:

- *The farmer in the dell* and *Three blind mice* (C major chord)

- *Coconut song* by Harry Nilsson (C7 chord)

Vamos a remar

One-chord songs

(A Spanish version of *Row, row, row your boat*)

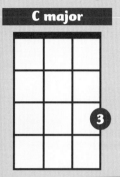

fingertips

● This song lends itself perfectly to the 'swing shuffle strum' — a down-up-down-up finger strum with the bouncy rhythm used in jazz 'swing' music or in folk dance 'jigs'. If you keep repeating the words 'Humpty Dumpty' from the famous nursery rhyme, you have got the swing shuffle rhythm:

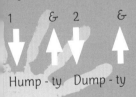

1	&	2	&
Hump - ty		Dump - ty	

C throughout

Va - mos　　a　　re-mar,

En　un bo - te-ci　-　to,

Rapido, rapido, rapido, rapido,

En　un bo - te-ci　-　to.

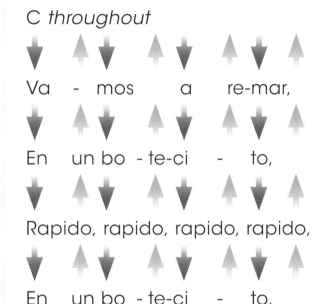

English words

Let's go rowing,
In a little boat,
Rapidly, rapidly, rapidly, rapidly,
In a little boat.

9/10 On track

● After a 2-bar introduction the song is played through twice, separated by a 2-bar interlude.

● It is then played again, this time in two parts as a 'round'.

11

Challenge

● Now you know the English and Spanish versions of this song, see if you can find versions in other languages.

● Perform this song as a round in two or even three groups. To do this, each group should start from the beginning when the group before reaches 'En un botecino'.

Songfacts

Different versions of the song can often be found in several countries. This version of *Row, row, row, your boat* is from Spain.

One-chord songs

Tongo

(A Polynesian Canoe Song)

1st time

  (taps)

C • • •

Ton-go

2nd time

 C

C

Ton-go

fingertips

Here are two possible ways to play *Tongo*:

● Play the C string with a thumb rest stroke on beat 1. Tap the ukulele on beats 2, 3 and 4.

● Play the C string with a thumb rest stroke on beat 1. Thumb brush strum the C major chord on beats 2, 3 and 4.

C throughout
Tongo,
Tongo.

Jimne baye, baye oh,
Jimne baye, baye oh.

Oo   alay,
Oo   alay.

Mah le ka   loa way,
Mah le ka   loa way.

11 / 12 On track

● After a 4-bar introduction, the song is played twice.

● First time: The solo singer is accompanied by the ukulele players picking the open C string and tapping the body of the instrument.

● Second time: an 'echo voice' is added, and this time the ukulele players pick the C string and thumb strum the C major chord.

Challenge

● Try singing *Tongo* in a group as an echo song, as demonstrated on the track: a leader sings each line for everyone else to echo. It's good fun.

Songfacts

Polynesia (meaning 'many islands') includes the Pacific islands of Hawaii and Tahiti.

This canoe song helped to keep the rowers in time and it can be sung as an 'echo song'.

One-chord songs

Ah, poor bird

A minor

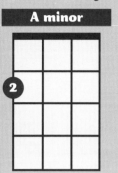

2

VERSION ONE

Ah, poor bird, take your flight,

Far above the sorrows of this dark night.

VERSION TWO

Ah, poor bird, take your flight,

Far above the sorrows of this dark night.

fingertips

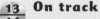

● Use a gentle thumb brush strum for this song. One strum at each Am chord symbol will be enough as it is not a song that needs a strong, rhythmic backing.

13 14 ● **On track**
● There are two versions of this song. You will hear four strums before the first version and a repeated strumming pattern before the second.

13
● Version two is played twice through, as a round.

Challenge

● Try playing version 2. The pattern is very simple; first play the open strings, A and E, then strum the A minor chord.

● Try singing the song in a group as a 'round'. The second group should start when the first reaches 'take your flight'.

Songfacts

This sad song is from Tudor times, about 500 years ago. In those days a song may not have been written down until long after it was first sung, so we often do not know the name of the composer.

Fly away

One-chord songs

F major

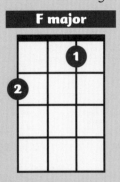

fingertips

- The song is written in a Caribbean style and is best accompanied on the ukulele using the Calypso strum.

- Use the TAB notation provided on the CD to play the melody for the instrumental verse or as the second part in the 'round'.

F *throughout*

Why do pel - i - cans fly   a- way,

Fly   a- way,   fly   a- way?

Win-ter comes and they fly a- way,

Fly   a- way   to Ja – mai -   ca.

Calypso strum

1 (+) 2 + (3) + 4 (+)

15 16 **On track**

- After a 4-bar introduction the song is sung through once.
- Then there is an instrumental verse before the song is sung again as a round.
- There is a short 2-bar interlude between repeats.

Challenge

- In a group, sing the song as a round (as demonstrated on the track).

- Play the tune of the song using the TAB notation (on the CD) as a 'round' for an excellent ukulele duet.

Songfacts

The song is about the annual migration of the brown pelican every winter from North-West America to the warm island of Jamaica.

Engine number nine

(An American railroad song)

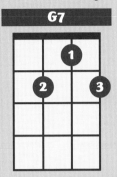

G7

fingertips

● Play the introduction nice and strong. Notice how the strumming pattern gets faster and faster like a train speeding up.

● For the ending, the pattern is reversed as the train slows down.

● Use the 'swing shuffle strum' for the song. It needs to be very rhythmic but not too loud.

INTRODUCTION

G7

SONG

G7

Engine, Engine Number Nine,
Rolling down Chicago Line,
If the train should jump the track,
Do I get my money back?

Swing shuffle strum

G7

En-gine, En-gine

ENDING

G7

17 / 18 **On track**

● The track starts with 12 percussion beats before the introduction begins.

● The song is heard three times, with an introduction between each repeat

● The second time is an instrumental verse, with the ukulele playing the melody.

Challenge

● Have a go at playing the melody line on the ukulele using the TAB sheet on the CD.

Songfacts

Many American railroad songs have been inspired by the sounds of a steam train.

In this arrangement, the G7 chords in the introduction pick up speed like a steam engine puffing faster and faster as it leaves the station. At the end the train slows down.

UNIT 3
TWO-CHORD SONGS

SIX SONGS TO SING AND PLAY

Strum, strum, strum, strum!

Uku-luku-lele! (the Hokey cokey)

I saw three ships

Dans la forêt lointaine

Water come a me eye

We've got the whole world in our band

In this section you will:

- Play six songs that each use two different chords
- Practise changing smoothly from one chord to another without hesitating
- Practise different strumming patterns
- Practise songs that can be sung in two parts (where both the verse and chorus can be sung at the same time)
- Practise a ukulele 'action song'
- Sing a song in French
- Have the opportunity to play the tunes of two songs (see TAB sheet)

Things to remember:

- Practise the chord changes slowly and smoothly before beginning each song.
- Avoid looking at your fingers on the fretboard as you change chords. Fingers will soon learn to make the chord shapes and feel their way around the frets. Practise changing the chords with your eyes closed.
- Keep your fingertips just above the strings.
- Remember that you may not have to move every finger to make a chord change. Instead of lifting a finger off a string completely, you may be able to slide it along.

This section supports these Units of the *Ukulele Magic Tutor Book*:

- *Strum, strum, strum, strum!, Dans la forêt lointaine* and *Water come a me eye* – Unit 5 (All change)
- *Uku-luku-lele* and *I saw three ships* – Unit 6 (Three chord tricks)

Check it out!

Here are some two-chord children's songs to try:

- C major and G7: *London Bridge, My hat it has three corners, This old man*
- F major and C7: *The wheels on the bus, Old Texas, Michael Finnigan, Hush little baby*

Strum, strum, strum, strum!

Two-chord songs

A minor | F major

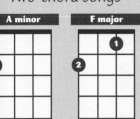

fingertips

● 'N.C.' means 'no chord'.

● Play the repeated chords with strong strokes and the first finger down.

● Damp the strings with the palm of your hand when you have strummed the four repeated chords

🖐. Allow the very last chord in the song to ring.

N.C.   Am   N.C.   Am

1. Strum, strum, strum, strum! ▼▼▼▼ When you're feeling blue,
2. *Ukulele solo*
3. Strum, strum, strum, strum! ▼▼▼▼ When you're feeling down,

N.C.   F   N.C.   Am

(1.) There's a way to go, ▼▼▼▼ Something you can do: ▼▼▼

(3.) Let it raise you up, ▼▼▼▼ When you hear that sound, ▼▼▼

N.C.   F   N.C.   Am

(1.) Get a ukulele. Strum, strum, strum, strum!

(3.) Of a ukulele, Strum, strum, strum, strum!

---

19 / 20 On track

● The track starts with four drum beats followed by a 4-beat phrase from the band.

● There is an instrumental verse (ukulele solo) between verses one and two.

● To end, the last 'Strum, strum, strum, strum!' is repeated twice.

Challenge

● Play the melody of the song using the TAB notation provided on the CD.

Songfacts

This song is in the style of classic blues guitarists like Muddy Waters. Check out his song *Boom, boom, boom, boom!*

Uku-luku-lele!

Two-chord songs

(The hokey cokey)

F major   **C major**

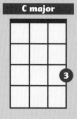

VERSE

N.C.
You turn your

Shuffle strum

fret - board in,   your fret - board out.

F
fret - board in,   your fret - board out.

F   C
In, out, in, out, shake it all about.

         C
You strum a ukulele and you turn around.

C   F   N.C.
That's what it's all about!

CHORUS

F   C
Oh uku-luku-lele! Oh uku-luku-lele!

F   C   F
Oh uku-luku-lele! Ukulele fun, strum, strum!

On track 21/22
● After a 2-bar introduction, the song is heard three times. The second time is instrumental and could include actions to go along with the strumming.

Challenge
● Extend this song with new words and actions for the ukulele.
● Try playing the three-note bass 'run' that links the verse to the chorus. (C, D, E)

Songfacts
The song is a ukulele version of the popular action song the *Hokey cokey*, with uke-appropriate actions.

I saw three ships

(An old English Christmas carol)

F major

C major

F   C   F   C

I   saw three   ships come sail - ing in,

F   F   C   C

On Christmas day, on Christmas day.

F   C   F   C

I   saw three   ships come sailing in,

F   F   C F

On Christmas day in the morning.

fingertips

● Lift all of your left-hand fingers cleanly and quickly away from the strings when you change between the F and C chords. Don't lift them too high!

● This is quite a lively song, so practise it slowly at first without the backing track.

23 24 On track

● The song is played three times:
First time: sing and play
Second time: play
Third time: sing and play

● Each verse has a 4-bar introduction (F C F C).

Challenge

● Play the tune of *I saw three ships* using the TAB notation provided on the CD.

Songfacts

The earliest printed publication of this cheerful little Christmas carol dates back to the 17th century.

There are several theories about where the ships were going and whom they were carrying.

Two-chord songs

Dans la forêt lointaine

(A French children's song)

F major   **C7**

VERSE

    F   F   C7   F
Dans la for-êt loin-taine on en-tend le cou-cou.

    F   F   C7   F
Du haut de son grand chene il repond au hibou.

CHORUS

   F   F   C7   F
Coucou, coucou, coucou hibou, coucou.

   F   F   C7   F
Coucou, coucou, coucou hibou, coucou.

fingertips

● The strumming pattern on the track uses very simple up and down finger strokes on each chord.

Strumming pattern

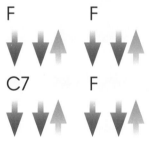

F   F

C7   F

25/26 **On track**
● After a 4-bar introduction, the song is sung through once, and then repeated as a part song, with a second voice beginning when the first voice reaches the chorus.

Challenge
● Try singing this song in two parts: one group sings the verse while the other group sings the chorus. It fits together very nicely.

Songfacts

This is a little French children's song about a cuckoo and an owl singing to each other in a faraway forest.

The two-note cuckoo call features in many pieces of music. For instance, in *The carnival of the animals* by the French composer Camille Saint-Saëns there is a section called 'In the heart of the forest' that features a cuckoo call played on the clarinet.

Water come a me eye

Two-chord songs

C major   **G7**

VERSE

C		C		G7		C

Ev-'ry time I re-mem-ber Li - za, wa-ter come a me eye.

C		C		G7		C

When I think about my gal Liza, water come a me eye.

CHORUS

C		C		G7		C

Come back Liza, come back gal, water come a me eye.

C		C		G7		C

Come back Liza, come back gal, water come a me eye.

fingertips

● This is the ideal song for playing the calypso strum we learned in the *Ukulele Magic Tutor Book*. The rhythm of the first five notes perfectly match the 'down, down-up, up-down' pattern.

● Later the rhythm of the song is different from the strumming rhythm. This can be quite tricky to play at first, but soon the calypso strum will feel natural and automatic.

Calypso strum

C

↓ ↓ ↑ ↑ ↓

Ev - 'ry   time   I   re-

27/28 On track

● There is a two-bar introduction before the verse.

● The song is first played as written; then it is played again as a round – with the second group starting when the first reaches the chorus.

Challenge

● Sing the song in two groups, as a round: when the first group reaches the chorus the second begins the verse.

Songfacts

This is a well-known folk song from the island of Trinidad in the Caribbean, which has been recorded many times by various artists.

We've got the whole world in our band

C major

G7

CHORUS

	C		C

We've got the whole world in our band.

        G7   G7

We've got the whole world in our band.

        C   C

We've got the whole world in our band.

        G7   C

We've got the whole world in our band.

VERSE

                C   C

1. We've got some Mexican marimbas in our band.

                G7   G7

We've got some Mexican marimbas in our band.

                C   C

We've got some Mexican marimbas in our band.

                G7   C

We've got the whole world in our band.

Strumming pattern

C

whole   world ...

VERSES

2. We've got some Russian balalaikas in our band ...
3. We've got some samba drums from Rio in our band ...
4. We've got Hawaiian ukuleles in our band ...

fingertips

● Stop and damp the strings for two beats at the end of each verse leading in to the chorus.

29/30 On track

● After a short introduction the song starts with a chorus.
● After the chorus, the four verses are sung, before finishing with a final chorus.

Challenge

● Write your own verses. You could include other instruments from around the world, for instance; 'We've got some steel pans from Tobago' or 'We've got mbiras from Zimbabwe'.

Songfacts

This song is a light-hearted adaptation of the well-known American gospel song *He's got the whole world in his hands*.

UNIT 4
THREE-CHORD SONGS

SIX SONGS TO SING AND PLAY

Happy birthday

Gospel medley: *I'm gonna sing, When the saints go marching in, Swing low sweet chariot*

Third fret blues

The more we get together

In this section you will:

- Play six songs using three different chords
- Practise changing between three different chords smoothly and without hesitating
- Sing a medley of three songs to exactly the same chord pattern, or 'sequence'
- Learn a new strumming pattern – the 'waltz strum'
- Have the opportunity to play the tune of a blues song (see TAB sheet)

Things to remember:

- Before playing each song, practise the chord changes slowly and smoothly.
- Break it down: practise changing from C to F, then F to G7, and then G7 to C before you put the whole sequence together. Be patient. It may not be easy at first but the chord changes will soon feel natural.

This section supports Unit 6 (Three chord tricks) in the *Ukulele Magic Tutor Book.*

Check it out!

Here are some more three-chord songs you could try, using only the chords C major, F major and G7:

- *Auld lang syne* (Traditional)
- *The lion sleeps tonight* (Solomon Linda)
- *Supercalifrigilisticexpialidocious* (from *Mary Poppins*)
- *Surfin' USA* (The Beach Boys)
- *Rockin' all over the world* (Status Quo)
- *Three little birds* (Bob Marley)

Happy birthday

Three-chord songs

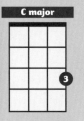
C major

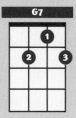
G7

F major

```
        C              G7
Happy birthday to you,

        G7           C
Happy birthday to you!

        C              F
Happy birthday dear  Mary

        C        (G7) C
Happy birthday to   you!
```

fingertips

● This song has a metre of three, with three beats to each chord. Use strumming pattern 1 to start, then try adding up-strokes for pattern 2.

● The G7 in the last line needs fast fingers! Practise changing between G7 and C slowly to get the hang of it.

Strumming pattern

1. Happy birthday to you …

2. Happy birthday to you …

On track

● After a 2-bar introduction, the tune is played twice, first with the down strums only and then with all strums.

24

Challenge

● You can change the name of the birthday boy or girl and play along with the backing track.

● This song is quite low-pitched because we are using the chords we know. You can raise the pitch of a song without learning to play new chords by using a little gadget called a 'capo'. Do some research, or ask your teacher to show you how to use a capo.

Songfacts

This song dates back to the late 19th century. It is based on a song called *Good morning to all* by two American sisters; Patty and Mildred J Hill.

It was written for the children in Patty's nursery school class.

Gospel medley

(1. I'm gonna sing / 2. When the Saints go marching in / 3. Swing low, sweet chariot)

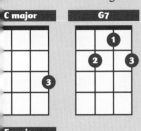

C major G7 F major

C

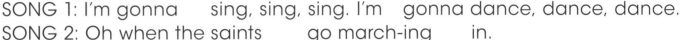

SONG 1: I'm gonna   sing, sing, sing. I'm   gonna dance, dance, dance.
SONG 2: Oh when the saints   go march-ing   in.
SONG 3: Swing   low,   sweet   cha   -   ri - ot,

                              G7

I'm   gonna   sing; I'm gonna dance, Allelu.
Oh when the saints   go   marching   in.
Coming   for   to   carry   me   home.

              C   F

When those gates are open wide, I'll be standing by your side.
I   wanna   be   in   that   number,
Swing   low,   sweet chariot,

                C   F   C

I'm gonna sing. I'm gonna dance,   Allelu.
When the   saints   go   marching   in.
          Coming for to   carry me   home.

fingertips

● Damp the strings for two beats to make a break between each song.

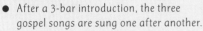

33/34 On track
● After a 3-bar introduction, the three gospel songs are sung one after another.
● The songs are then repeated, this time as a medley in three parts, with each part starting when the one before reaches Song 2.

Challenge
Try singing this medley in up to three groups:

● The second group should begin when the first group has reached the second song, and the third follows the second.
● Listen carefully to the track and have a go!

Songfacts
This is a combination of three well-known African American gospel, or 'spiritual', songs.

They can all be played using exactly the same sequence of chords and can also be sung at the same time.

Third fret blues

Three-chord songs

(A blues song to sing and play)

C   C   C   C
Any time I wanna play the blues,

F   F   C   C
It's the ukulele that I choose,

G7   F   C   C
Third fret is the only one I use.

Strumming pattern
C

A -ny time I

fingertips

● Choose a simple strum like a 'swing shuffle' (↓↑↓↑) to accompany the song. Use a soft thumb brush strum to accompany the ukulele solo; it is important not to drown out the solo instrument. Musicians refer to this as 'keeping out of the way'.

35 / 36 **On track**
● After a 2-bar introduction the song is sung once with ukulele accompaniment.
● Then the melody is played as a ukulele solo.
● Lastly the song is sung again with some ukuleles strumming the chords and others picking out the melody.

26

Challenge

● Create your own solo using the 'blues' scale. Check the song *Playing the blues* in the *Ukulele Magic Tutor Book* for information about improvising with the 'blues' scale.

● Play the ukulele solo verse using the TAB notation. It may look complicated but the whole thing can be played using open strings and notes found at the third fret.

Songfacts

Blues music developed in the USA from African American call-and-response work songs or 'field hollers' as they came to be known.

A classic blues song has three lines, or musical 'phrases', of equal length: the melody (and often the lyrics) of the first two lines is exactly the same, though the chords are different.

The third line often has a different melody and lyrics.

The more we get together

Three-chord songs

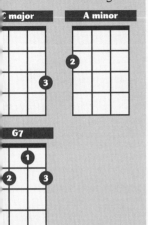

C major   A minor

G7

C   Am   G7   C
The more we get to - gether, to - gether, to - gether,

C   Am   G7   C
The more we get together the happier we'll be.

G7   C   G7   C
For your friends are my friends and my friends are your friends.

C   Am   G7   C
The more we get together the happier we'll be.

Strumming patterns

1. Simple strum

C   Am   G7   C

2. Waltz strum (for instrumental)

C   Am   G7   C

fingertips

- The simplest way to strum this song is to play down-strums on each chord (pattern 1)

37 / 38 On track

- After a 2-bar introduction, the song is played three times. The first and third times use a simple down-strum (pattern 1).
- The second time is an instrumental verse; listen out for the Waltz strum here.

Challenge

- You could adapt the words of the song to make it more personal to you and your friends at school: 'For Kofi is my friend and Kofi is your friend'.

Songfacts

This is a 19th century American children's song which has been used in many other songs including *Did ye ever see a lassie*.

It has even been quoted in several pieces of classical music.

UNIT 5
FOUR-CHORD SONGS

FOUR SONGS TO SING AND PLAY

Oh Christmas tree

The leaving of Liverpool

Nkosi Sikelel' iAfrika

Walking bass

In this section you will:

- Play four songs using four different chords
- Have the opportunity to play three ukulele solos (see TAB)
- Sing a song in African languages

Things to remember:

- The chord changes should be broken down and practised separately before playing the whole song.
- The more chords you know, the more songs you can play.

This section supports and extends Unit 6 (Three chord tricks) in the *Ukulele Magic Tutor Book.*

Check it out!

Here are some more four-chord songs you could try using only C major, A minor, F major and G7:

- *Ob-La-Di-Ob-La-Da* – The Beatles
- *Baby* – Justin Bieber
- *All I have to do is dream* – The Everly Brothers
- *Stand by me* – Ben E. King

Oh Christmas tree

Four-chord songs

(O Tannenbaum)

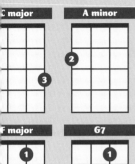

C major A minor

F major G7

C   Am

Oh Christmas tree, Oh Christmas tree,

  G7   C
Your leaves are so unchanging.

    C   Am
Oh Christmas tree, Oh Christmas tree,

  G7   C
Your leaves are so unchanging.

    C   F
Not only green when summer's here,

  G7   C
But also when it's cold and drear.

    C   Am
Oh Christmas tree, Oh Christmas tree,

    G7   C
Your leaves are so unchanging.

fingertips

● Use the same three-beat strumming pattern as in *Happy birthday:*

39/40 **On track**

● After a short 4-bar introduction, the song is played three times. The second time through is an instrumental verse.

Challenge

● Invent a new strumming pattern by using a rhythm that appears in the song several times. You could use the rhythm of the words:

Christmas tree, Oh Christmas tree

Songfacts

This was originally an old German song dating back to the 16th century.

It was called 'O Tannenbaum', which means 'fir tree'.

The leaving of Liverpool

Four-chord songs

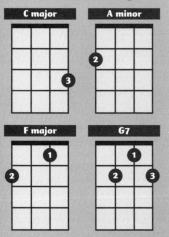

C major   A minor

F major   G7

fingertips

● Use this strumming pattern throughout the song:

1   2   &   3   4   &

● Leave a little break between the verse and the chorus by 'damping' the strings 🖐 after beat 3 of the strumming pattern. This is written in the music as 'N.C.'

VERSE

     C   Am   F   C

⬇️ ⬇️⬆️⬇️ ⬇️⬆️⬇️ ⬇️⬆️⬇️ ⬇️⬆️

Farewell to   Prince's Landing Stage,
      C   Am   G7
River Mersey fare thee well.
      C   Am F C
I am bound for California.
      Am   G7   C
It's a place that I know right well.

CHORUS

N.C. G7   F   C
So   fare thee well my own true love;
      C   Am   G7
When I return united we shall be.
        C   Am   F   C
It's not the leaving of Liverpool that grieves me,
      Am   G7   C
But my darling when I think of thee.

41 42 On track
- After a 4-bar introduction, the first verse and chorus are sung.
- This is followed by a ukulele solo verse, before the chorus is sung again.
- After the chorus, a final verse and chorus is sung.

Challenge
- Play the ukulele solo verse using the TAB notation on the CD.

Songfacts

This famous folk song was almost certainly a 'capstan sea shanty' – a work song sung by sailors as they turned the capstan on a 19th century sailing ship.

It is a sad song about embarking on a journey and leaving loved ones behind. It became very popular in Ireland because many poor Irish emigrants, forced out of their homeland by a terrible famine, boarded ships at Prince's Landing Stage in Liverpool to cross the Atlantic Ocean to America.

Nkosi Sikelel' iAfrika

(God bless Africa)

A minor   **C major**

G7   **F major**

Am   C   G7   C

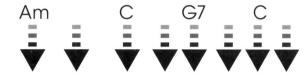

Nkosi sike - lel' i - Af – ri - ka,

C   F   C   G7

Maluphakanyisu 'phondo lwayo,

Am   C   G7   C

Yizwa imithandazo yethu,

F   C   G7   Am

Nkosi   sikelela,

F   C   G7   C

Nkosi   sikelela.

English translation

God bless Africa,
May her spirit rise up high,
Hear thou our prayers,
Lord bless us.

finger tips

● Use a simple thumb brush strum on the beat and concentrate on clean chord changes; there are only two strummed beats on each chord.

Challenge

● Play the ukulele solo using the TAB notation on the CD.

● Check out the full version of *Nkosi Sikelel' iAfrika* and listen to some of the many recordings that have been made.

43/44 On track

● After a short introduction, the song is played three times: the first time is sung, the second is a ukulele solo, and the final is sung again.

● The ukulele solo is written as a 'descant' line three notes (or a 'third') higher than the original tune. A TAB version is available on the CD.

Songfacts

This song was written in a poor neighbourhood in South Africa in 1897 by a Methodist schoolteacher, Enoch Sontonga, for his congregation to sing. He wrote the original words in Xhosa – the African language of the local people. He set the words to a Welsh hymn tune which he adapted.

For many years in South Africa it was an anthem of resistance to apartheid. It now forms part of the national anthem.

There are many versions of this song and it has been extended to include verses in other African languages. The lines in this short version are written in both the Xhosa and Zulu languages.

Walking bass

Four-chord songs

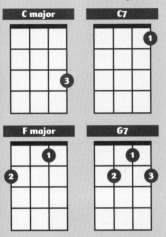

C major   C7

F major   G7

45
46

fingertips

● Try a Swing shuffle (↓↑↓↑). It is an ideal accompaniment for this type of jazz-style music.

● Remember not to strum the chords too heavily during the ukulele solo. You could strum each chord once in the solo verse to help lighten up the backing.

C   C
If you like your music jazzy

C   C7
Add a walking bass.

F   F
Keep it simple, nothing snazzy,

C   C
Now we're talking bass.

G7   F
You can do it, nothing to it;

C   C
Play that walking bass.

Swing shuffle strum

C

If   you   like your ...

On track

● After a 2-bar introduction the song is heard three times, with a ukulele rendition the second time.

Challenge

● Play the ukulele solo using the TAB notation provided on the CD.

● Remember to use only one finger for each fret.

● This piece is not only a fun ukulele solo, it is a great workout for the fingers.

Songfacts

This jazz song uses almost the same sequence of chords as *Third fret blues* and *We're playing the blues* in the *Ukulele Magic Tutor Book*, with the addition of the C7 chord.

It also includes some other features of jazz: the 'walking bass line' and also the 'boogie-woogie' swing-style accompaniment.